Where They Go in Winter

Written by Rachel and Ari Mintz
Illustrated by Damian Radulovic

Where They Go in Winter

Written by Rachel and Ari Mintz
Illustrated by Damian Radulovic

They don't even know it, but frogs are quite cool.
Their body temp changes to match that of the pool!

They feel fine with no coats, but still get a bit frozen.
Their bladders and bodies and skin are those chosen.

The rest of them stay nice and thawed through the season.
That's 'cause of a chemical that prevents total freezin'!

Because they're so cold, they stop movin' and groovin'.
Which means that they don't need to take as much food in!

When the weather gets warm, their bodies do too.
They start hopping and plopping right back up to you.

Trout are cold-blooded, just like those frogs.
All winter they're under thick ice in their ponds.

Some chill out with their friends, others swim solo.
They don't eat that much and they move real slow.

Mallard Ducks have to escape the cold.
Otherwise they'd have no more food to behold.

Ice traps some food beneath the water,
while snow hides the rest—such a bother!

Mallards fly to warm places like Cali.
Or Ole Miss, if they don't like the Valley.

Snakes go anywhere free from the frost, otherwise
they'll freeze and soon after they're lost!

They like holes and caves, woodpiles too,
and sometimes they'll bid other critters adieu!

Once they're inside, they slow way way down.
They're not asleep, just not able to clown.

Those that ate before entering the den
will survive the winter and slither again!

Rabbits will hide in bushes and piles of leaves—anything
so another animal won't see.

Some even change colors to be more grey and white, matching
the landscape—a winter delight!

They'll still sneak out to gather their food.
They just gotta be careful to stay un-viewed.

Squirrels like to hang with their friends in the winter.
They stay in their dens—and boy do they shiver.

They quiver and shake with all their might,
which helps them stay warm and snuggly at night!

Squirrels prepare for the winter all fall,
eating and hiding some food from their haul.

On their bodies they build up nice layers of fat,
so they don't have to venture far from where they're at.

They also have all that food squirreled away,
that they can dig up for more energy to play!

Wolf spiders are cold-blooded, just like the trout.
When the temperature drops, they don't like to go out.

They burrow underground to stay toasty and snug.
So they can hunt later - that's a good bug!

Just like the squirrels, racoons store their food.
They want to chow down when they're in the mood!

Racoons store fat in their striped racoon tails,
for more insulation if the furnace fails.

They stay anywhere that gives them a haven—
whether a tree, others' dens, or a cave-in!

Mice are resourceful, seeking shelter indoors.
Like the kitchen, garage, or even your drawers!

Because they're so warm, not much changes for them.
They eat and they play 'til again and again.

Black bears go to brush piles, under trees, and caves, too. For 8 months they don't even poo!

Bears hibernate, so they sleep winter away.
And their pee turns to protein—so no need for whey.

Their fat and their coats keep them all warm and toasty. They like to fly solo and be alone, mostly.